# Wakefield

## IN OLD PHOTOGRAPHS

The new bridge opened on 1 June 1933, in Wakefield's 'Year of Progress'. It replaced the Chantry Chapel Bridge which was built in the 1340s as Wakefield's main route south across the Calder.

# Wakefield

## IN OLD PHOTOGRAPHS

Compiled by
CHRISTINE JOHNSTONE

Alan Sutton Publishing Limited
Phoenix Mill · Far Thrupp · Stroud
Gloucestershire

Published in collaboration with

Wakefield Metropolitan District
Council Leisure Services: Museums,
Galleries and Castles.

First published 1993

Copyright © Wakefield MDC, 1993

**British Library Cataloguing
in Publication Data**

Johnstone, Christine
Wakefield in Old Photographs
I. Title
942.815

ISBN 0-7509-0333-3

Typeset in 9/10 Sabon.
Typesetting and origination by
Alan Sutton Publishing Limited.
Printed in Great Britain by
Redwood Books, Trowbridge.

# Contents

# Introduction

In 1800 Wakefield was an important market town, home to about eight thousand people. Situated at the very edge of the Pennine foothills, Wakefield benefited from being on the border between the textile towns to the west and the coalmining villages and farming communities to the south and east. In 1800 there were still no railways or motorways, just turnpike toll roads and the Aire and Calder Canal. Canals carried bulky freight efficiently and economically – wool, corn and lime into the West Riding and cloth, coal and stone out of it.

Wakefield's main industries included textiles, grain processing, wholesale livestock sales and, outside the town, farming and coalmining. Indeed the land between Wakefield and Leeds was described as 'black with pits' in the 1770s. Unlike Bradford, Wakefield had too few fast-flowing streams to power much of the new water-driven textile machinery. Instead local firms concentrated on finishing processes – fulling, dyeing, raising the nap on cloth, or cropping it with giant hand shears. Wakefield's livestock market was large and successful. Cattle and sheep from Lincolnshire, the East Riding and the Skipton district were sold to butchers from as far afield as Halifax, Huddersfield, Sheffield and Manchester. In the early nineteenth century, industry expanded into new sites near water – typically, Westgate End, Thornes and Belle Isle. However, Wakefield did not grow on the spectacular scale of the more purely textile towns like Leeds and Bradford.

By 1835 the Calder was 'crowded with sturdy sloops, laden in bulk to the water's edge'. The river banks were an 'emporium of grain . . . studded on both sides with buildings of magnificent dimensions'. In the same year over 170,000 sheep and 13,500 cattle were sold at the market. In 1840 the railways came to Wakefield when the Manchester and Leeds Railway Co. opened Kirkgate station.

Industrial expansion was matched by other changes. In 1800 Wakefield had few civic institutions; by 1860 it had many: the Court or Session House (designed 1806), the Music Saloon almost next door (opened 1823), the Mechanics Institute (1841), a comprehensively rebuilt prison (1848), the town's first hospital (1853), a new enclosed market (1856) and a new station at Kirkgate (1857). In 1865 Wakefield held its own Industrial and Fine Art Exhibition, fourteen years after the original one at London's Crystal Palace. The exhibition attracted 189,000 visitors in just forty days.

On the edge of town new rows of brick houses sprang up. Some, like St John's Square and South Parade, were of the highest quality; others in Primrose Hill, Eastmoor, Thornes and Belle Vue were much poorer and meaner. At the same time the town centre gradually filled up with slums. The backyards and gardens behind the main streets became cluttered up with rubbish heaps, pigsties and slaughterhouses, all next to overcrowded houses with outdoor toilets and open drains.

In 1848 Wakefield had become a borough, and in 1888 it was made a city. A year later Wakefield became the administrative centre of the new West Riding County Council – a compromise that both Sheffield and Leeds could tolerate. This new role had a great effect on Wakefield, not least along Wood Street, but probably also encouraging the development of theatres (the Opera House in 1895, the Empire in 1909), rugby teams, public parks and much much more.

Industrial growth was quite slow, but by 1900 railways, factories and warehouses had taken over large areas of land in Thornes and Calder Vale. Men worked in engineering, mining, iron working and chemicals, women mainly in textiles – a common pattern in the West Riding. Some of the major firms in 1902 included E. Green & Son, Joseph Rhodes & Sons, Bradley & Craven, Charles Roberts, Alfred Ellis, M.P. Stonehouse, Spurr Inman & Co., the Seamless Steel Boat Co., British-Jeffrey Diamond and Kilner's. With the introduction of steam power and even electricity, textile spinning had become important locally, with over 104,400 spindles working in Wakefield in 1912–13.

By 1910, 23,694 people lived in the city, whose boundaries had been extended out to Alverthorpe and Sandal. An extensive horse-bus and then electric tram system developed to connect the once-separate old villages and the new suburbs like Belle Vue with the city centre.

After the First World War, the new County Borough of Wakefield enjoyed new and extensive powers. One result was a massive house building scheme to replace some of the extremely poor housing in the city centre with brick-built semis with gardens. Portobello was the first such estate, home to families from Pincheon Street and Volunteer Yard, east of Kirkgate. The wonderful new houses had two bedrooms, a living room, a scullery containing a bath covered by a table top, a larder and an outside toilet. Lupset followed three years later in 1924, Darnley, Eastmoor and Thornes Road were started in 1930 and Flanshaw and Peacock Farm in 1936. Kettlethorpe, the first out-of-town estate, was only started in 1951.

The year 1933 was designated Wakefield's 'Year of Progress'. Part dream, part reality, at a time of high unemployment and great poverty, the year celebrated both the new modern bridge over the Calder and the morale-boosting pageant. As well as the historic scenes acted out at Clarence Park, the Wakefield Pageant also included a carnival parade, a race for old cars, a railway exhibition at Westgate and a shop window treasure hunt.

For civilians in Wakefield, the main effect of the Second World War was the departure of many men and women to the armed forces and other forms of war service. Wakefield itself suffered very little bombing compared with

London, the ports and some of the big industrial cities. Everyone was involved in rationing however, which started in January 1940. While it caused a lot of paperwork, inconvenience and disruption, rationing undoubtedly improved the diet of the poorest families in Wakefield and elsewhere. It continued into the austerity period after the end of the war – bread finally came off ration in July 1948 and clothing in March 1949. Rationing was finally and completely lifted in 1953, to coincide with the Queen's coronation.

Wakefield has probably changed more rapidly in the last forty years than at any time in its history. Streets like Kirkgate have been redeveloped not once, but twice, in the mid-1950s and again in the early 1980s. Small family-run shops and businesses have been replaced by national chains and multinational companies. Society has become much more car-based and regional in outlook, and people think nothing of commuting long distances to work each day. Wakefield is now the focal point of a population spread out as far as Crofton, Stanley, Outwood and Crigglestone, as well as the administrative centre of a metropolitan district stretching as far as Knottingley, Ossett and South Elmsall.

It is precisely because of Wakefield's changing history that photographs of the city and its people are so important. Maps can show the roads and paths, prints and sketches record the pretty or the picturesque, but only photographs show us the everyday. This book includes formal studio portraits from the 1870s, busy street scenes from the 1900s, civic photographs from the 1930s and street panoramas from the 1950s. All help us understand the kaleidoscope of changing tastes and fashions that have made up Wakefield.

The book is divided into ten sections, covering many different aspects of everyday life. 'Around the Town Centre' takes you on a walk down Westgate, into Thornes Lane, up Kirkgate, along Wood Street and back to Warrengate. 'Memorable Events' covers royal visits, carnivals, ceremonies and the happy day in April 1946 when Wakefield Trinity won the Rugby League Challenge Cup. 'Home, Sweet Home' takes you from the late-medieval timber-framed homes to the high-rise flats of the 1960s, with their spindly furniture and dazzling wallpaper.

'Wakefield in Wartime' looks at the role of civilians in the 1914–18 munitions factories, and the 1939–45 Home Guard and ARP, as well as recording the damage caused by air raids in 1940 and 1941. 'All Change' looks at some of the buildings we have gained, and some we have lost, between 1904 and 1963. Some of the local occupations recorded in the section on 'Work' include blacksmith, farmer, shopworker, shopfitter, printer, servant, builder, teacher, nurse, warder and fireman.

'Buses and Trams' records Wakefield's first public road transport, while 'Shopping' looks at many long-gone emporiums such as Tansley's in Westgate, Preston's in Northgate, Benson's in Cross Square and Raper's in Kirkgate. 'Leisure and Sport' records the parks, clubs, pubs and religious organizations that local people supported, plus the football, rugby and swimming teams. Finally the section on the 1933 Wakefield Pageant looks both backwards and forwards, finishing with an imaginative view of Wakefield's youth of the future.

# SECTION ONE

# Around the Town Centre

Silver Street in 1900, seen from the junction with Wood Street.

The Black Swan, Silver Street. The buildings on Silver Street itself have long since been turned into shops, but the pub still uses the eighteenth-century premises in the yard.

Walking down Westgate in the 1880s, shoppers passed Tansley's at No. 80 and then Hinchcliffe's at No. 84.

The Great Northern Railway was keen to impress its competitors with the splendour of Westgate station. It opened in 1867, and is still in use, but these buildings were demolished in 1967.

Wakefield Prison, *c.* 1912. It was largely rebuilt on 'modern' lines in the 1840s, with cells facing on to corridors for easier control of the prisoners. The government took over control of the prison in 1878.

Westgate, *c.* 1900. With so many horse-drawn vehicles, public water troughs were quite a common sight. This one was near the junction with Ings Road.

The cattle market on Denby Dale Road was sold to the council in 1938. It finally closed in 1963 after 198 years in business. Now only the nearby Graziers pub on Market Street remains.

Looking upstream along the cobbles of Thornes Lane Wharf in the 1920s. These houses were in frequent danger of flooding.

A car peeps out from Casson Row on to Thornes Lane Wharf. Mills and malt-houses line the Portobello bank of the Calder.

Road-building at the Kirkgate end of Thornes Lane in the 1960s.

Traffic on Chantry Bridge, *c.* 1905. The woman is pushing her bike into town, while the tram is heading south. The John Smith's pub standing between the Doncaster and Barnsley roads is the White Bear Hotel.

Bridge Street and Tootal Street, *c.* 1925. In the Second World War this was the site of a deep bomb-shelter.

Steam traction-engine on the bridge, *c.* 1895. In May 1901, 5,304 horse-drawn vehicles, 3,530 bicycles, 15 motor cars and 8 traction-engines were counted using the bridge in just four days.

Chantry chapel was built in the 1340s and heavily renovated in 1847–8. Within forty years the smoke and grime from factories and mills had already damaged the new pinnacles.

At the bottom of Kirkgate in the 1920s. A policeman stands at the road junction while, in the centre background, a crane unloads cargo from an unseen barge moored at the weir.

A busy day in Kirkgate in the same period as the previous photograph. A motor bike and side-car race down between the tramlines.

Walking up the west side of Kirkgate in May 1964, the shopper passed Kayes, Gallons, Crockatts and George's.

After George's came Wiley's and Reliance Motors. Reliance were the Mercedes Benz main dealers but also sold Standard Triumph cars.

The shopper then continued up Kirkgate to Wool King and Malcolm's, passing many long, narrow yards on the way.

After Malcolm's came the Progress Stores, Halfords and the Criterion Hotel.

Scarrs, Morton's, Dewhurst's and the Double Six pub.

Dodging the Kirkgate traffic to reach Hiltons and Cavendish. Primrose House is on the skyline.

Hiltons, Timothy White's and the Kettering and Leicester Boot Company. Pickles' tailors and outfitters, next door, was where the boys went from the Queen Elizabeth Grammar School to buy their uniforms.

The corner of Kirkgate and Warrengate, 1909. Stephenson's furniture shop and the Dolphin pub had just been rebuilt after road-widening.

Upper Kirkgate on 5 May 1955, before redevelopment. On the left are Philip Taylor's, Driver's Stores and the Fifty Shilling Tailors.

Looking back down Upper Kirkgate on the same day as the previous photograph.

All Saints' parish church became Wakefield Cathedral in 1888. In this 1933 photograph the noticeboard in front of the spotlights appeals for £600 for restoration work.

A horse-bus turns from Northgate to Kirkgate, opposite the west (tower) door of the Cathedral. The city's horse-bus service ran from 1890 until just after the trams were introduced in 1904.

Butcher's Row, a narrow lane, was widened in 1909. This changed Cross Square from a square into a street leading to the Cathedral.

The Grand Clothing Hall, built in 1906. After the 1909 alterations, it dominated the new view from the Bull Ring corner to the Cathedral.

Wood Street transformed the town in the nineteenth century with four grand civic buildings – the Mechanics Institute (now the museum), the Town Hall, the Court House and the City Hall.

Outside the Town Hall, 1957. It's 5.30 p.m., work has just finished, and people are queuing to get the Bradford bus home.

Northgate and Providence Street on 3 September 1951. This corner was soon to be swept away in the extensive redevelopment of the town centre.

A choice of drinks on Northgate, opposite the Bull Ring, 23 July 1939. Thirsty shoppers could choose between Miss Briggs' café, the Griffin Hotel and the Regent Café.

Warrengate, c. 1907. HP Sauce is still with us, but what has happened to Benefit Shoes and the North British Railway?

# Memorable Events

Seven sets of twins are certainly memorable, but the identity of these children remains a mystery. Six pairs are identical twins, the sister and brother at the bottom right being the odd ones out. The children posed in a Kirkgate studio in 1912.

A gigantic bonfire, built at Sandal Castle for King George V's coronation in 1911. Like many other cities, Wakefield celebrated royal coronations with enthusiasm.

Party time in Belle Vue for King George VI's coronation in 1937. Some of the boys look decidedly miserable!

King George V and Queen Mary visited Wakefield on 10 July 1912, during their tour of the industrial north. The royal couple spent twenty minutes at E. Green & Sons, where the workers' families waited to see them in the factory yard opposite a large model of Green's famous 'Economiser'. The workers themselves are out of view in a grandstand on the other side of the yard.

The King and Queen visited Newmillerdam, Cradock's wire-rope works, Green's, and the Seamless Steel Boat Co. before lunching at Nostell Priory. In the afternoon they drove across the city on their way to Ossett.

The crowds fill Kirkgate, at 3 p.m., waiting for a glimpse of royalty. St George's cross and the Union Jack flutter from every building.

Between factories the King and Queen passed a group of miners wearing the latest emergency breathing apparatus. Although mines rescue stations had been made compulsory in 1911, Wakefield's own station did not open until 1914.

King George V spent twenty minutes at the Seamless Steel Boat Co. in Calder Vale Road. The company's boats were pressed out in two halves and then riveted along the keel.

Wakefield's local Queen, 12 July 1938. The mayor, Alderman T. Crowe, greets the new Rag Queen, Miss Amy Wood, on the Town Hall steps.

The mayor and the Rag Queen were later the victims of a hoax 'stick-up', raising funds for hospital charities.

Alverthorpe had its own carnival, and probably its own Carnival Queen. This is the procession of 1906.

At the other end of town, and in about the same year, these young girls were dressed up for the Sandal and Belle Vue Carnival.

The Bull Ring is packed out as the mayor unveils the memorial to Queen Victoria in 1905. The statue was moved to Clarence Park in 1950 and returned in 1985.

Rather fewer people made up the invited audience who attended the opening of this memorial on 28 September 1910.

The crowds stare as the clergy leave the Cathedral by the tower door, after a service of dedication for the new St Mark's chapel on 15 April 1905.

A procession from the Town Hall to the Cathedral in February 1946. The new Bishop of Wakefield, the Rt Revd Henry McGowan, is being enthroned.

The crowds are so deep at this Wakefield procession that one of the floats is lost in the middle.

The soldiers march in rank, but the crowds in Wood Street press on them from every direction. A man and a young boy look on from a window above Dyson's shop, while two other men have climbed the lamp-post.

Just one policeman seems enough to control the crowds in the late 1930s. Perhaps the rain has dampened enthusiasm!

Trade carts helping to raise money in the Lifeboat Procession on another rainy day, this time in 1895.

A different way of fund-raising: racing with mechanical horses at a Wakefield fête.

Children in costume at the opening of the Wakefield Labour Party's Bazaar in December 1938. Middle row, left to right: -?-, Councillor Effie Crowe (mayoress), Mrs Greenwood, -?-, the Rt Hon. Arthur Greenwood MP, Alderman T. Crowe (mayor).

Inspecting the Christmas post, December 1938. Mayor Crowe, the mayoress and other dignitaries make the traditional visit to the Wakefield sorting office.

A Christmas party in December 1945, with the mayor Cllr Effie Crowe and the mayoress, Mrs Winifred Ashton. War has only just ended, and food is still rationed.

Wakefield Trinity won the Rugby League Challenge Cup in April 1946, beating Wigan in a closely fought match. Here the mayor and mayoress congratulate Trinity's captain Billy Stott.

Wakefield Trinity parade the Rugby League Challenge Cup through the town on their way to a civic reception. They travelled from Westgate Station to the Town Hall in a Beverley Brothers lorry trimmed with red and blue ribbons, as the Wakefield Old Band played 'See the Conquering Heroes Come'. The team was mobbed by an excited crowd all the way from the station platform to the Town Hall steps.

Wedding splendour, 8 July 1903. When Sarah Abson married Ernest Williams, wide hats, trailing bouquets and Bo-peep crooks seem to have been all the rage.

Changed fashions, 10 August 1926. Mr J.K. Thompson and the former Miss Sybil Crowther after their wedding in Wakefield Cathedral.

# SECTION THREE
# Home, Sweet Home

The first high-rise flats appeared on the Wakefield skyline in the early 1960s. The first tenants moved into Carr House, just off George Street, in 1961.

The Six Chimneys in Kirkgate. Many pre-industrial buildings were later converted to shops on the ground floor and family homes above.

Bond Terrace, built in 1840–1.
Wakefield's first terraced houses were
substantial homes for middle-class
families.

Terraced houses sprang up all around the city centre in the 1880s and '90s. Some had
bay windows and railed gardens, others opened straight on to the street. This postcard
was sold to proud new residents of College Grove Road.

Park Lodge Lane still had a semi-rural feel in the 1920s. Houses of different sizes and shapes lay at odd angles to the road.

At the same time, nearby Marsland Terrace was unmistakably urban, with its parallel rows of identical houses.

Down a back lane off Primrose Hill, *c.* 1910. Houses like these lacked the bathrooms, electricity and central heating that are taken for granted today.

The Model Lodging House in Piccadilly was one of few places where single men, or men working away from home, could find a bed. Herbert and Lily Hemingway managed the house before it closed in 1937.

Homes fit for heroes. The council's house-building programme began in 1919. Over the next twenty years new estates opened up at Lupset, Peacock, Eastmoor and here at Flanshaw.

New houses continued to be built in the 1950s and '60s, often on the edges of the 1930s estates.

Neighbours chatting in Pannel Avenue, Eastmoor, on a sunny day in May 1960.

New homes and bare gardens in Starbeck Road, Eastmoor. In the 1960s architects still firmly rejected the grid-like pattern of earlier terraced housing.

High-rise flats were seen as a cheap and efficient way of rehousing a lot of people quickly. In 1962 Primrose House rose up out of a web of scaffolding at the bottom of Kirkgate.

Primrose House received its first tenants in October 1963. By this time the council had built 1,007 flats in Wakefield, mainly in smaller blocks at Eastmoor and Kettlethorpe.

Show flat in Carr House, early 1960s. The sitting-room included a sideboard, a coffee table and a coal-effect electric fire.

The dining-room boasted spindly shelves, a fitted carpet and a table for two.

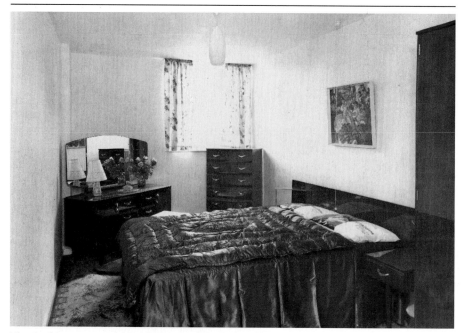

The bedroom was almost filled by the double bed, with its shiny eiderdown and the brand-new pillows still in their wrappers.

No room for dust or cobwebs: show flats encouraged new tenants to make the best of their new homes.

# Wakefield in Wartime

The Queen's Own Yorkshire Dragoons mobilizing for war in August 1914. The First World War saw cavalry soldiers like these pushed aside by the newly-invented tank.

Women and girls on war work at E. Green & Sons, Calder Vale Road. The woman in the centre with a large hat must have been a supervisor; all the others were on the production line. Munitions work was hazardous, but it provided higher wages and more independence than domestic service or mill work.

Filling shells by hand. The women wore mob caps to keep their long hair out of harm's way. Many factories converted to munitions production during both world wars.

Brass artillery shells lined up in a spartan workshop at Green's. Each young woman had responsibility for the 400 shells on her table.

Park Lane Auxiliary Hospital was set up with 100 beds in the County Hospital to treat soldiers injured in the First World War. Casualties were appallingly high in the trenches of northern France and Flanders.

Matron and her nurses pose with their two young mascots.

The County Hospital opened in 1899 to treat 'the sick poor of the working class'. This is one of the ten-bed wards transferred to the Auxiliary Hospital.

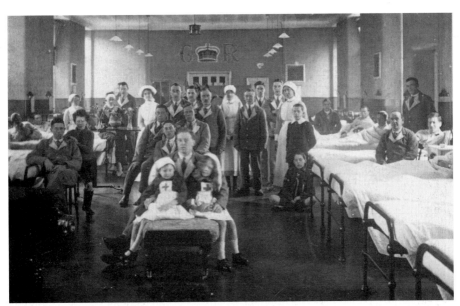

A large ward, decorated to honour King George V during the First World War. In all, 1,192 soldiers were treated at the Auxiliary Hospital.

Mr R. Beales and the Minerva. In 1939, this 36 hp car was converted from carrying game at Chevet to fighting fires in Wakefield. It was scrapped in 1941.

Building a sandbag shelter on the allotments in Balne Lane, between the railway bridge and the prison. When there was an air raid people hid in the cellar (if they had one), under the stairs or in a specially built shelter outside.

Wakefield ARP spray 1,500 gallons of water a minute across the Calder. This public demonstration took place at Thornes Lane Wharf in October 1938. It was meant to calm any fears about fire storms, should war be declared and the Germans bomb the big mills along the Calder. The ARP also hoped to attract new recruits.

The fire brigade do their bit for ARP recruitment. Mustard gas had been used in France in the First World War, so the government ordered everyone to carry gas masks in case of an attack. Fortunately they were never needed.

Home Guard volunteers relaxing at a Wakefield dinner. Many men who were unable to fight because of their age or their work joined 'Dads' Army'.

Air raid wardens from Eastmoor at Newmarket Colliery, Stanley, in March 1939. With local politicians, they are inspecting the new air raid shelters dug into the pit hills for surface workers at the colliery. Many of the men who lived in Eastmoor worked at Newmarket, or other local mines.

Wakefield's first air raid took place at Norton Street, Belle Vue, on 28 August 1940. It injured four people, destroyed six houses and seriously damaged eight more.

The second Wakefield raid, on 16 September 1940, produced no casualties, but demolished one house and damaged another. In the third raid, on 12 December, bombs landed on the prison and at Chantry Road, Lupset, but failed to explode.

Wakefield's worst air raid took place on 14 March 1941 at 10.50 p.m. Two large bombs fell on Thornes Road, one at the rear of No. 76 and one between Nos 48 and 50.

Six people died and four more were severely injured. All the houses between Nos 38 and 104 and between Nos 151 and 232 Thornes Road were damaged or destroyed.

Dutch children at the Town Hall in February 1946. In the last few months of the Second World War the Dutch were reduced to eating tulip bulbs as food supplies failed. After the war ended these 130 children were brought to Wakefield for two months to recuperate.

# All Change!

Speeches, music and bunting accompany the laying of the foundation stone of Wakefield's new Salvation Army barracks by the local MP on 27 July 1907.

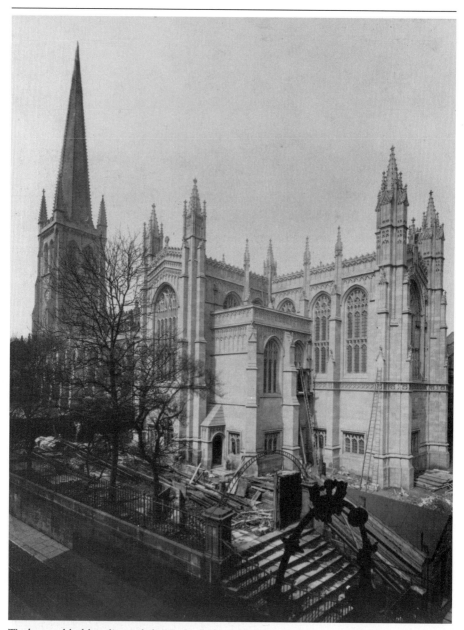

Timber and ladders littered the Cathedral yard as the work on the new extension neared an end in 1904. The new part of the Cathedral was built in memory of William Walsham How, the first Bishop of Wakefield.

The Bishop Blaize Inn was closed on 12 June 1924 and knocked down in 1926 to make way for a new road junction and railway bridge where Thornes Road and Denby Dale Road meet.

New Wells House was demolished in 1937 to extend Drake and Warters' shop-fitting works in Thornhill Street. One hundred years earlier sufferers from gout and from sore eyes had visited New Wells to use its two natural medicinal springs.

Lupset from the air, 1926. Curving roads and spacious gardens produced a totally new road pattern for working-class housing in Wakefield. To reflect this, the main road through the estate was romantically named after George a Green, the Pinder of Wakefield. Legend says that he fought with Robin Hood.

The ruined house of the Battys. In 1937 the West Ardsley firm of Crosland and Sons started to demolish some dilapidated cottages in Milner's Court, off Flanshaw Lane. Behind the frontages they found a sixteenth-century, oak-framed house. It had a 1541 date-stone, twenty-four rooms, four stone fireplaces and a large brick-built chimney-stack. Despite this, the house was still demolished.

Chantry chapel's new front. The renovations of the 1840s were destroyed by air pollution in just ninety years. The new west front was dedicated on 3 July 1940, but the restoration was not completed until after 1945. The design of the new front was the same as the one it replaced, but both of these were different from the 1340s original. A sculpture of the coronation of the Virgin Mary had been considered unsuitable by the 1840s and was replaced by one showing the descent of the Holy Spirit.

The Six Chimneys collapsed on the evening of 16 May 1941, after many structural alterations in the previous decades.

Empty space east of Northgate in May 1949. The bus station opened in the area to the bottom right of this photograph in 1952.

April 1953. The buildings at the corner of Northgate and Providence Street have all disappeared, to be replaced by temporary hoardings and a car park.

Cars parked on a demolition site on the east side of Kirkgate, 29 September 1953.

The crowds stare at the changes at Springs on 27 April 1955. Vicar's Croft, a disused graveyard, was making way for road-widening and a row of shops. A total of 146 cholera victims had been buried there between 1832 and 1849.

Kirkgate was comprehensively redeveloped in the 1950s. On 28 September 1955 the roofless remains of the George Hotel are still just standing opposite the Cathedral.

Four weeks later and the George has gone.

Lower down Kirkgate on the same day. The Beehive clings on amid the cleared site.

Early on a Sunday morning, 27 March 1956. Looking past the Bull and Mouth to the new shops.

Beyond John Colliers, The Beehive falls, 28 August 1956.

Little Westgate also faced redevelopment in the summer and autumn of 1956.

A parade of modern shops rising at the corner of Kirkgate in March 1957.

The Golden Cock Inn, at No. 31 Westgate, during demolition in May 1963. Although this richly carved, jettied building looked medieval, it is surprisingly late. It must have been built in the early seventeenth century, as recent research on tree rings in the wood has shown that the building's oak timbers were only felled around 1600. The original roof had gables facing the street.

Technical College extension, Bell Street. The first phase opened in 1962, but work on the new assembly hall, gym, library and lecture theatre only began in 1963.

Jackets off on a hot summer's day, Bell Street, early 1960s. It is easy to see why building work was so dangerous in the 1960s.

Slab by slab, Primrose House rises up at the bottom of Kirkgate. Ready-made sections speeded up the work on site and made the flats cheaper to build.

Only seven floors to go. Primrose House is just one of several identical eleven-storey blocks of flats built near the city centre in the early 1960s.

A mass of girders and flimsy scaffolding as the new market hall rises off Brook Street during the summer of 1963.

No way through. Shoppers take to the road past the building works on 15 July 1963.

The new market hall was built by the site of the century-old market hall. Stallholders continued to sell from the open stalls, minimizing disruption during the building programme.

Building the sewage works below Primrose Hill, on the east side of the railway line to Featherstone. A small railway track had been laid to bring materials to the site. As Wakefield's population grew and health standards rose, both the sewers and the water supply needed to expand to keep pace.

Laying new drains in the 1920s. Many roads in Thornes were disrupted when the new drains were laid to the Calder.

Sitting in the drainage pipe, to show how large it was.

Temporary road repairs in the 1920s. The trench has been filled and workmen pour hot tar on to the gravel before the steam roller gives it a smooth finish.

More holes in the road, again in the 1920s, but this time at the junction of Stanley Road and Eastmoor Road.

# SECTION SIX

# Work

Unloading coal for G. & J. Stubley's eight Lancashire boilers. Stubley's were woollen manufacturers at Calder Mills and Castlebank Mills in Portobello Road. Joseph Petch (standing on the quayside, seventh from the left) was scalded to death here in 1930 when a boiler pipe burst. Stubley's gave his job to his son.

Fred Wood, *c*. 1910. Mr Wood (on the left) kept dairy cows at Westfield Farm off Barratt Road, less then a mile from the city centre.

Mr Lancaster and two workmen at the blacksmith's forge, Ivy House, Agbrigg. In the age of the horse, the blacksmith was as important as the MOT garage is today.

Five grocers' boys outside a Wakefield shop around 1910. Shopwork meant long hours and low pay.

Drake & Warters were shop-fitters in Thornhill Street. For this photograph thirty-eight of their male employees posed with their flat-bed lorry in the 1930s.

A saddle-tank locomotive approaching E. Green & Son's factory in Calder Vale Road. Green's 'Economiser' recycled the waste heat from boiler chimneys.

Two carefully posed workmen using a crane and bogey at Green's. In 1900 the company employed about a thousand people.

Fourteen men working in one corner of Green's in 1895. The pulleys and cranes ran from rails hung below the ceiling.

Casting vertical tubes at Green's in the same year, with no protective clothing except flat caps and heavy boots.

A Female School of Industry opened in Almshouse Lane in 1818. Young girls learned craft skills to help them find work, and the school made money from what the girls produced. The Almshouse Lane school was the third of its kind to open in Wakefield. It closed around 1870 when the parish church school opened in Zetland Street. The building eventually disappeared under the Ridings Centre.

Eight women who worked at Nicholson's Albion Works in Vicarage Street in 1890. Nicholson's printed novels and reference books at the Albion Works between 1871 and 1921.

Printers and bookbinders, c. 1933. These men and women worked for John Lindley Son & Co. in the old Female School of Industry building in Almshouse Lane.

A woman working at Green's in the 1940s.

Protective gloves were worn, but otherwise there seem to have been few safety features.

Two women working on a different part of the engineering process.

Miss Anne Ashton, a paid companion to Miss Clarkson of Northgate in the 1870s. Between 1850 and 1910 many women worked in service. Their jobs ranged from the unseen kitchen maid to the constant personal companion.

Reynolds, Stott and Haslegrave, 1923. The company used the West Riding Mill in Thornes Lane and King's Mill at the end of the bridge. The first corn mills on the Calder used water power, but steam engines took over in the nineteenth century.

Alfred Haley & Sons, worsted spinners. Haley's were on the other side of the city, at Westgate Common Mill on Alverthorpe Road. In 1926 they were almost surrounded by fields and allotments.

The Close Asbestos and Rubber Co. was based in old wool warehouses at Nos 15–17 Cheapside. In the late 1920s the staff posed with sacks of Carco asbestos insulation products outside the Cheapside works.

A Beverley Brothers lorry outside their brewery in Harrison Street, off Thornhill Street. It has been decorated for Wakefield's Rag Day in October 1949.

Staff from Wakefield's Mines Rescue Station in 1927. From left to right: Walter Prattern, Arthur Shepperd, Alfred Dobson, William Riley, Oswald Kear, Bob Summerton, Fred Armitage. Behind them is their first call-out vehicle, a Fiat lorry.

Harry Hainsworth's team, working on a new sewage scheme along the Calder in the 1920s. Hainsworth was an engineering and public works contractor, based at Ings Road.

Lindsay Avenue, Lupset, in 1937. Construction of the estate began in 1924. From left to right: Ernest Lister, Albert Aveyard, Albert Morton, Dick Musgrave, George Armitage, Frank Harrison, Joe Day.

A woman teacher and the headteacher at Alverthorpe School in 1916. Boys sat with boys and girls with girls. Women were not normally allowed to carry on teaching if they married.

Wakefield School for Girls, 1941. Top row, left to right: M. Allen, M. Fennell. Middle row: J. Kingswell, M. Hutchinson, M. Bolton, P. Dewse. Seated: S. Rycroft, E. Wakefield, D. Town, Miss Clapham (teacher), N. Hall, E. Baines, J. Laverack. On the ground: J. Taylor, D. Clark.

Craft Room, St Michael's School. One teacher controlled over thirty pupils, without making them sit in rows facing forwards. St Michael's School opened on the site of Flanshaw Hall in 1951.

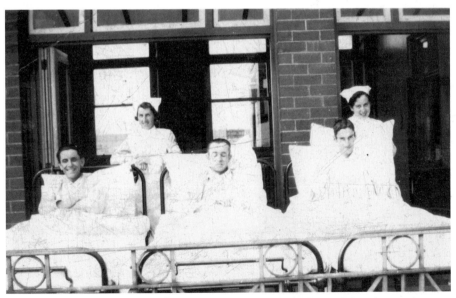

Nurses and patients at Snapethorpe Hospital, c. 1925. The isolation hospital was a necessity when poor housing made many people suffer from infectious diseases and chest diseases.

Twenty postal workers outside their Market Street headquarters in 1890.

Eleven prison warders outside the Love Lane entrance to Wakefield Prison, *c.* 1905.

Wakefield City Police outside the Drill Hall in 1922. Like most other urban areas, the city had its own police force until 1968, when it amalgamated with the West Riding force.

Wakefield's special constables, just before the 1968 amalgamation. George Senior, the Divisional Commandant, is fourth from the left on the front row.

Wakefield City Fire Brigade with its horse-drawn, steam fire-engine outside the Town Hall in 1894.

Engineer W. Adams, a Wakefield fireman between 1893 and 1937.

## SECTION SEVEN

# Buses and Trams

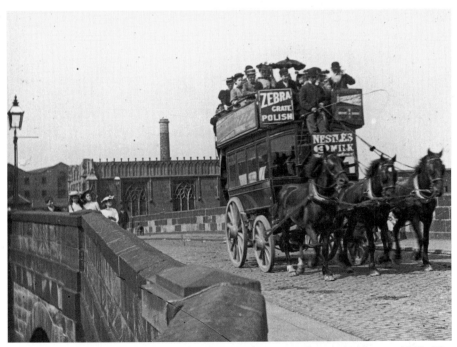

A crowded three-horse-power bus heading south across Chantry Bridge, *c*. 1900. The journey from Wakefield to Agbrigg was timetabled to take twenty-five minutes.

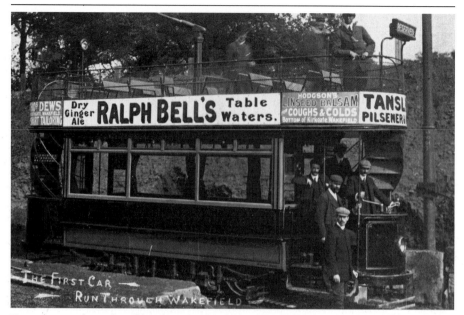

Fast, clean and comfortable, electric trams soon replaced the smaller horse-buses. There was great interest in the new transport system. Postcards were sold of this, the first tram through Wakefield, even though it was not yet in service.

Wakefield's first public tram service, at Newton Bar at 7.15 a.m. on 15 August 1904. Everyone wanted a ride that day, so the timetable was temporarily abandoned.

The first tram in the Bull Ring, 22 July 1904. Tram No. 13 was on a test run and although the indicator board shows Castleford, this route was never constructed. Castleford had its own separate tram system.

Another first, this time the first tram from Wakefield to Leeds. This photograph shows a church or chapel outing which seems to have chartered the tram.

Trams needed a high capital investment. Ornate electricity poles sprouted up from the pavements and the setts were dug up to lay rails. Here on Northgate in 1909 the tram service in each direction shared a common centre rail to reduce costs.

The Bull Ring in 1904. Two open-topped trams fill up with passengers, while three horse-drawn Hackney carriages wait quietly for fares.

A year or two later, and much has changed. Queen Victoria's statue is in place, the tram rails have been doubled, and tram No. 41 to Agbrigg is one of the new, roofed models.

The tram network spread right across Wakefield. This photograph shows a Sandal–Leeds tram passing the old toll-house at Newton Bar and the winding gear of Wrenthorpe Colliery, commonly known as Newton Pit. The pit re-opened in 1907 and finally closed in the late 1920s.

Westwards from Wakefield the Ossett trams ran on two sets of rails right down the middle of Westgate. Wakefield's last trams ran from Agbrigg to Ossett in July 1932.

Southwards a single tramline ran along Doncaster Road. Away from the town centre the electricity poles were much simpler and cheaper.

Outside the Griffin Hotel tram No. 10 waits to set off for Leeds. A similar tram
trundles across the Bull Ring, in front of six motor taxis. The police recorded this traffic
congestion in the 1920s.

Buses need neither rails nor electricity poles, but their running costs are higher than trams. Here a small single decker travels east along Westgate, past Thompson's Yard.

Another single-decker motor bus, this time in Cross Square on a snowy lunchtime in the mid-1920s. Wakefield's first motor buses appeared in 1922.

Leyland Lion LT1 bus, 1930. Longer buses could carry more passengers but cost more to buy and run.

Where there's a bus-stop, there'll probably be a queue! Twelve would-be passengers wait outside the old Registry of Deeds in Kirkgate on 27 July 1953. This is now the site of Woolworths.

# SECTION EIGHT

# Shopping

Westmorland Street, August 1939. With demolition scheduled, the drapers Hague Brothers offered a great clearance sale before their move to the other side of the Bull Ring.

For wines and spirits, try J.W. Tansley's West Riding Wine Stores, at No. 80 Westgate. Their stock in the 1890s included port, sherry, hock, Australian wines and Glenlivet.

Tansley's sold ale and stout at 2s. 6d. for a dozen pints, plus their own brand of whisky – TOG, or Tansley's Old Genuine.

Lewis Hughes' Italian Warehouse, the Bull Ring, 1964. South African sherries, cocktail mixers and much, much more were available. The business was established in 1785 and taken over by Mr Hughes in the late 1920s. The business continued on the same site after this building was knocked down in August 1964.

J.E. Hinchliffe sold butter, margarine, chocolate, cocoa, bacon, stout and wine at No. 84 Westgate in the 1890s.

Butcher's boys wait for work outside the Shambles, also in the 1890s. Fourteen old back-to-back butchers' stalls stretched between Cross Square and the Bull Ring, no doubt creating all sorts of hygiene problems.

Preston's were at Nos 38–40 Northgate for at least fifty years. Originally they dealt in game and poultry, and then expanded into fruit. This view was taken on 3 July 1950.

Prizewinning display of English cheeses in a Wakefield shop-window. The Stilton had 'real delicacy and perfect flavour' and was 'sure to please'.

Many German families set up food shops in West Yorkshire from the 1880s onwards. Here in Northgate in 1921 Hagenbach's, the bakers, stood next to Ziegler's, the pork butchers. Other local pork butchers of German origin included Paul Andrassy, Charles Hofmann, William Oesterlein and William Weegmann.

For many years Benson's confectionery shop and Webster Brothers' refreshment rooms were neighbours in Cross Square. Websters also ran grocery shops at No. 202 Kirkgate and at No. 70 Westgate.

A busy shopping afternoon on the corner of Cross Square and the Bull Ring in the 1920s.

Woolworths opened their new shop in 1956. There has been a branch in Kirkgate since before 1922.

Simpson's shoe shop, at the corner of Westmorland Street and Brook Street, on 24 March 1940.

Hiltons' shoe shop, at the corner of Almshouse Lane and Kirkgate, opposite the bottom corner of the Cathedral. The windows are piled high with the new season's footwear.

William Hannan's newsagents opened in 1891 at No. 1 Butcher's Row, between Cross Square and Northgate. This ancient timber-framed building was knocked down in 1909 and the business transferred to new premises nearby.

Hobson's sweet shop, Little Westgate, *c.* 1920. The window is full of crackers, stockings and other Christmas novelties.

Mrs Phoebe Storr ran a newsagents and tobacconists at No. 103 Westgate. Her 1904 advertisement promised newspaper delivery to any address in the city.

Bartle Brothers, *c.* 1910. These stationers and printers were at No. 100 Westgate and Nos 5–7 Drury Lane for many years. The site is now a car park.

C. Turner & Sons, No. 5 Wood Street, *c.* 1910. The pillars, mouldings and signs on the shop front advertised the firm's skills as signwriters and decorators.

H.T. Raper & Son in the 1960s. The firm had been in Kirkgate for over eighty years. For a long time their shop at No. 196 Kirkgate concentrated on ironmongery and the one next door at No. 198 on china.

The Borough Market was built in 1865. By the early 1900s the twenty-eight indoor stalls sold meat, sweets, hats, ironmongery, butter, eggs and books. Outside you could buy flowers, fruit, potatoes, vegetables, fish, underwear, hats, haberdashery, tobacco, china, cloth and tripe, or visit the blacksmith or the herbalist. On a quiet day in the 1890s the choice seems to be between potted plants and wallpaper.

# Leisure and Sport

The Belle Vue Palace Cinema opened in 1914 and closed in 1960. It was known as 'the spit and whistle' because of two large signs at either side of the screen – 'Do Not Spit' and 'Do Not Whistle'.

The Hippodrome opened in Teall Street in 1903 as a venue for 'equestrian and variety entertainment'. The first films seen in Wakefield were shown at the Hippodrome in 1907 and from then till its closure in 1922 it was used solely as a cinema. The building was auctioned in 1923 and ended up being moved to Brandy Carr and used as a rhubarb-forcing shed.

The Empire Theatre, later the Gaumont, opened in Kirkgate in 1909. It was converted to a cinema in 1921. *Up Front* and *Cattle Drive* were showing on 13 September 1951, just before the redevelopment of this part of Kirkgate.

The Gaumont British Junior Club for Boys and Girls, December 1947. The cinema club was celebrating its second birthday.

Mr W. Harold Smith as Blicky Bill in the Wakefield Amateur Dramatic Society's 1929 performance of *The Belle of New York*. Wakefield had a strong amateur dramatic tradition for many years.

Dressed very differently, Harold Smith took on the role of Pomeral in *The Girl in the Taxi*, which the society put on two years later.

Latin American glamour at the theatre in the Amateur Dramatic Society's performance of *Rio Rita*.

A member of the Wakefield Sylvian Operatic Society in a very different costume drama.

An exhibition of riding and hunting at Holmfield House in the 1930s. Wakefield Museum was based at Holmfield House from 1923, and eventually moved to Wood Street in 1956.

Afternoon tea in the garden of No. 88 Batley Road, 1905. The Glover family could afford to employ servants, and so these sisters enjoyed a fairly leisurely lifestyle.

Four generations of Absons, Alverthorpe, 1912. Back row, from left to right: John Burton, Walter Stubley, Ernest Williams, J.M. Abson, his son Israel Abson, John Roberts. Middle row: Marjorie Williams, Sarah Williams, Hannah Abson, Martha Stubley, Ellen Burton. Front row: Miranda Abson (later Mrs Roberts), Ernest Harold Williams, Esther Abson. Hannah and Israel were the parents of Sarah, Martha, Ellen, Miranda and Esther.

Exploring Sandal Castle, *c.* 1910. The Parliamentarian army destroyed this thirteenth-century stone castle in 1645, and it was only excavated in 1964–73.

Happy days in New Scarborough, along Alverthorpe Road, 1933. When homes were small, families large and fast cars infrequent, children happily played on street corners. At least one of the girls has been left to look after a younger brother or sister.

Enjoying the sunshine in Sandal Park, *c.* 1910.

The new Clarence Park bandstand opened in 1926 during the General Strike. It replaced a smaller one inconveniently placed on the top of the hill. The stage is shell-shaped, to throw the sound forwards.

The Black & White Dance Band at the Music Saloon (now Wakefield Museum) in 1926. Ronnie Pearson played saxophone, Alfred Horton, drums, George Carter Milner, violin and Alec Smith, piano. The Music Saloon had a sprung dance floor upstairs.

Another concert group from the 1920s.

A Bible class for young men based at the Methodist chapel, Doncaster Road, around 1920. The young man in the pale suit was William Price. Many people spent much of Sunday at religious meetings and services.

Members of Wesley Hall Sunday School marching through Lupset. Wesley Hall replaced a wooden army hut erected at the corner of Thornes Lane and Horbury Road in 1928.

Among the tulip beds in the 1920s. A member of the Wakefield and North of England Tulip Society points to his carefully grown tulips. The feathered and flamed patterns treasured by society members originate from a harmless virus carried by greenfly.

Annual Show, 1920s. The Wakefield Society was founded in 1836 to breed and show the old English florist tulip. Then just one of many such societies, it is now the only one left.

With their billycans and staffs, these young Belle Vue scouts seem ready for adventure.

Scouting in Wakefield. The founder of the scout movement, Lord Baden-Powell, visited Wakefield and Pontefract in 1933 and 1937.

Roller-skating at the Olympia Rink soon after it opened on 15 May 1909. The building, on the corner of Ings Road and Denby Dale Road, could hold up to 1,500 spectators and 300 skaters. A pianola-organ provided the background music.

From 1874 to 1938 Wakefield's only public baths were at Almshouse Lane. A second baths, at Sun Lane, opened in 1938, complete with a stage at the back for theatricals.

Almshouse Lane Baths, 1930s. As tin baths and outdoor toilets became less common, swimming and fun at the baths became more important than bathing and washing.

Sandal church's soccer team in 1916/17.

Wakefield City's soccer team in 1901. Back row, from left to right: E. Clarkson,
W. Gravitt, C. Newsome, E. Atkinson, W. Bennett, D. Hague. Middle row: E. Milsom,
C. Harrison, I. Burrows, J. Green, F. Hodgson. Front row: C. Bennett, F. Gill.

Wakefield Cricket Club in 1880. The club's only professionals, Firth and Elliott, played
in almost every game, unlike the amateurs. The best batsman averaged 22 runs an
innings, and the best bowler got 13 wickets for 77 runs.

Wakefield Trinity, *c.* 1892. This team played amateur rugby union. Players were first compensated for their missed wages in 1895, allowing ordinary working men to become regular team members. The professional league followed soon after.

Wakefield City Police rugby team, Christmas 1920.

The Cross Keys Inn on Bread Street was just one of 118 pubs and hotels in Wakefield in 1904. There were also three temperance hotels. Everyone was trying to get into this picture, including a man upstairs in the pub. The Cross Keys themselves referred to St Peter and to the arms of the see of York, which included Wakefield when the pub opened in the early 1800s.

There was a wide choice of pubs in Kirkgate in the 1950s. The Old Ship was just above the railway bridge. Today a home improvements centre lies on the site.

The Wellington Hotel, a Beverley Brothers pub at No. 174 Kirkgate, on 20 February 1959. The Eagle Brewery was just behind the pub, in Harrison Street.

The Criterion Hotel on 7 May 1964. The upstairs of this John Smith's pub extended over the entrance to Chadwick's Yard from Kirkgate.

The Double Six, still serving Sam Smith's Taddy Ales in May 1964. Soon it would disappear with the redevelopment of Kirkgate.

The Bishop Blaize on Stocks Hill, Thornes. The pub was named after the patron saint of woolcombers, reflecting the importance of the worsted industry in Wakefield. It closed in 1924 and was knocked down two years later.

Driving out of town along the Horbury Road in the 1950s, drinkers had a choice between the Redoubt and the Robin Hood.

# The 1933 Wakefield Pageant

Crowds at Westgate station welcoming the special train bringing visitors from Leeds. The 1933 pageant was organized by the Chamber of Trade to encourage trade.

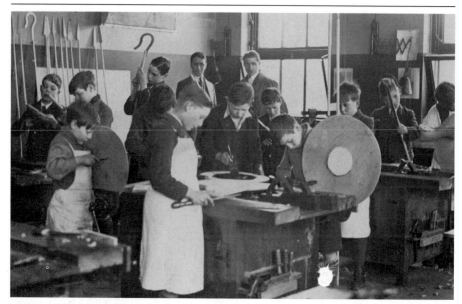

Making shields and spears, Snapethorpe School.

Boys from St Austin's, lined up at the Technical School with their shields.

Pupils from Thornes House Grammar School also making preparations. At all these schools, woodwork was seen strictly as a boys' lesson.

Local art students designing the pageant costumes. Special emphasis was placed on historical accuracy.

Katherine Leach, the elected Pageant Queen, and her maids of honour. The eight attendants were C. Gillat, M. Hemingway, E. Brewer, Joan Whittle, M. Ward, D. Churchill, A. Carrs and I. Gelder.

The rehearsal in Clarence Park in front of a cut-out model of the grammar school. Directly or indirectly, three thousand people took part in the pageant's eleven episodes.

Practising to be Elizabethans at the rehearsal.

Snapethorpe Juniors rehearsing at school in their Puritan costumes.

Representing 'Merrie Wakefield', the participants await their call at the dress rehearsals. The Elizabethan episode was 'a riot of colour and high spirits'.

Ancient Britons, but perhaps with more than a passing influence from Honolulu.

Ancient Britons and their Roman captors. In the first full episode of the pageant, the Britons were disarmed and taken away under escort.

The early episodes included the Prologue, the Ancient Britons, the overthrow of paganism, the Norman Conquest and Robin Hood's fight with the Pinder of Wakefield.

The Saxons' helmets bear more than a passing resemblance to pit helmets.

Good Queen Bess, played by Mrs Crook, with her attendants in the Elizabethan or Alverthorpe episode.

Schoolchildren from St Mary's, St John's and the Cathedral Girls' Schools. Some of the boys appear reluctant to wear the lace and fancy clothes of the 1600s and 1700s.

John Nevison holding up a coach in Westgate. Ledgar Goldsworth played the notorious highwayman. Other episodes covered industry, the 1897 Jubilee and the suffragettes.

Mrs Haig as the reforming spirit of the nineteenth century. She welcomed women coming out of the mines with the words 'England is mighty, Britain rules the waves, Let not our ships be launched in tears of slaves; Arise! Rejoice, and shake your fetters free – Then hail thy England, land of liberty.'

Market women in the Mystery Play episode. But what is a native American Indian woman (left) doing in medieval Wakefield?

Wakefield's youth of the future in the pageant Prologue. They got the miniskirts and the jumpsuits almost right, but, oh, those hats!

# *Acknowledgements*

I wish to express my sincere thanks to everyone who has given or lent photographs to Wakefield Museum since the 1920s. Without their generosity neither this book nor the museum's collections would be as comprehensive as they are. I would also like to thank my colleagues in Wakefield Museums, Galleries and Castles, particularly Gill Hall, Mark Hall and Gordon Watson, for their help, support and encouragement.

Many of the photographs in this book were taken for Wakefield City Council. The numerous individuals and organizations who gave or lent photographs included here are listed below, together with page references.

Mr Adams: 102a. Mr C.J. Baines: 108. Mr R. Beales: 58a. Mrs E.J. Colbeck: 104a, 105a, 107a. Mrs G. Copley: 91a. Mr Dimsdale: 130a, 130b, 131a. Mrs E. Earnshaw: 102a. Mr M. Evans: 87a. Mr K. Farrar: 118. Mr David Firth: 58a, 133. Miss Amy Gill: 28b, 33a, 54, 55a, 55b, 85, 104b, 145. Green's Economiser Group: 29, 88a, 88b, 89a, 89b, 92a, 92b, 93a. Mrs Haig: 141b, 142a. Mr Haigh: 111a, 111b, 119b, 127, 129a. Mr R. Hainsworthy: 63a, 63b, 71a. Mr Jack Harness: 60b. Mr Frank Harrison: 68, 97b. Mr B. Hemingway: 47b. Mrs A.E. Jackson: 93a. Mrs Lancaster: 86a. John Lindley Son & Co.: 91b. Mr H. Longbottom: 110a. Miss W. Morgan: 16a. Mrs M. Oddy: 101b. Mr Ronnie Pearson: 137a. Mr Charles Pickles: 67a. Mr Eric Raper: 47a, 82. Mrs E. Robinson: 137b. Mr D. Shortland: 123a. Mr J. Stanley: 138a. Mr Arnold Taylor: 98a. Mrs M.B. Topliss: 131b. Mr Turner: 124b. By courtesy of the *Wakefield Express*: 41, 64, 95b. Mr D. Watson: 135b. Mr Webster: 119a. Mr E. Williams: 42a. Miss M.M. Williams: 135. Mrs Wiseman: 144a. By courtesy of the *Yorkshire Observer*: 99a. By courtesy of the *Yorkshire Post*: 40b.